FIRST EDITION
ISBN: 978-0-578-62007-7

This book would not exist without:

Mackenzie Keck's design eye and generous advice

The Rothko Chapel's art and holy books

Sarah Montonchaikul's love

THE
LITTLE
BOOK
OF LOVE

TRANSCENDENT TEXTS

THE KITÁB-I-AQDAS

The Most Holy Book in Bahá'i was written by its founder Bahá'u'lláh', in 1873 while he was imprisoned in the city of 'Akká. It was then supplemented with replies to a series of questions posed by one of His secretaries.

THE ANALECTS

Known as the "Analects of Confucius," the ancient Chinese book is composed of the sayings and wisdom of Confucius and his contemporaries. It was compiled and written by Confucius's followers during the Warring States period from 475 BCE to 221 BCE.

THE TORAH

Judaism's holy book, it tells the story of the Jewish people, their trials, covenant with G-d, and way of life laid out as moral and civil laws. It was written by the prophet Moses around 400 BCE.

THE BHAGAVAD GITA

Sanskrit for "Song of God," the text was composed by Vyasa in the 1st or 2nd century CE, and is an episode of the great poem of the Hindus, the Mahabharata. It takes the form of a dialogue between Prince Arjuna and the god Vishnu incarnated as Krishna.

THE TAO TE CHING

The fundamental text of Taoism, The Tao Te Ching is an ancient Chinese text written by the sage Laozi in 6th century BCE. It's written in a poetic style and in two parts; the Tao Ching and the Te Ching.

THE DENKARD

Compiled in the ninth century, it contains quotes and materials thousands of years older. It's considered an encyclopedia of the Zoroastrian religion, not it's sacred text, which is The Avesta.

THE QURAN

The central and most holy text of Islam, the Quran is the word of God as transmitted through his Prophet Muhammad. Written in 609 CE, it contains 114 chapters organized by length of it's passages called Surahs.

THE AGAMAS

Following tradition, the text was orally passed down from one generation to the next for millennia. The collection of truths uttered by Jain Arahas and written by disciples was then compiled and codified in the 5th century CE.

THE BIBLE

The divinely inspired Christian Bible contains sacred scriptures of historical accounts, hymns and allegories that make up the Word of God. It's a combination of two parts written in the 2nd century BC and the first century AD.

THE TRIPITAKA

Meaning "three baskets," this collection of teachings on Discipline, Discourse, and Doctrine, was composed around 550 BCE. The central text of many forms of Buddhism, it was passed down orally for generations before being put on paper.

THE GURU GRANTH SAHIB

The principal scripture of Sikhism was written by the religion's ten gurus, and the text itself is the final, eternal-living guru. It's 1,430 angs are poetically written to the rhythm of an ancient north Indian form of music.

Sacred Symbols

NINE POINTED STAR

The number nine is significant in Bahá'í for many reasons. These include it being the highest digit, it's numerical value being the word "Bahá'í," and it symbolizing Bahá'í's place as ninth and most recent in the line of "existing religions."

WATER CHARACTER

Though Confucianism has multiple symbols and no official one, the Chinese character for "water" is often used. This is because it represents the "source of life," as well as calmness and serenity, two things important to Confucianism's goal of harmony.

OM

The Om is the visual representation of a sacred sound considered to be the greatest of all mantras. Following the Hindu belief that existence began with sound and frequency, the symbol is considered to represent the essence of the universe.

YIN YANG

The perfect circle represents the Tao, the unity out of which existence arises. Second, it's two interconnected and balanced colors represent the two interdependent forces that together manifest the world.

FARAVAHAR

The word Faravahar translates into "I choose," and it's symbol serves as a reminder for us to live a good life. It's different parts have many meanings, culminating in a visual metaphor for humanity choosing good reflection, good words, and good deeds.

STAR AND CRESCENT

The commonly acknowledged symbol of Islam, it rose to prominence with the Ottoman Empire, and has no scholarly sacred meaning. However some believe the moon represents the seasons of the Islamic calender, and the star the five pillars of Islam.

AHIMSA

The hand and word in the center
represent Ahimsa, the core tenet of
Jainism to do and intend no harm. The
Dharmachakra wheel symbolizes the
desire to stop the cycle of reincarnation
through Ahimsa.

LATIN CROSS

While there are several variations of
the Christian Cross, the Latin Cross
is the most universially recognized.
It represents the crucifixion of Jesus
Christ, the son of God and savior
of mankind.

STAR OF DAVID

This symbol, carefully chosen to
represent the Jewish faith and people,
was taken from the powerful and
mystical Seal of Solomon, the signet
ring worn by King Solomon, and the
shield of King David.

DHARMACHAKRA

Used in many Indian Religions, this-Dharmachakra represents the Buddha's Dharma — the cosmic law and order and teachings of Buddha. It can also represent the Four Noble Truths, the Noble Eightfold Path, and Dependent Origination.

KHANDA

The Khanda is an amalgamation of three symbols depicting different weapons, including crossed swords symbolizing temporal and spiritual power. All together it represents Deg Tegh Fateh, the call to provide food and protection for the needy and oppressed.

   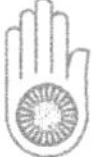  

Dear Reader,

I am honored and a little surprised you are here.
I pray you can forgive me. I don't think I don't deserve it.

It's true that I came to these sacred texts with my best;
an earnest yet uneducated attempt at the reverence and
respect they are so clearly owed, and that countless
believers have beautifully shown.

However, I can see now that what I set out to do was very
likely impossible, and very probably destined to offend. I just
haven't spent the lifetimes in study, community, prayer, and
contemplation needed to know if this is something that can
even be done. If it can, then I definitely don't have the
education, and mastery of both ancient and modern
languages required to do it correctly.

And yet, something in me felt called to create it.
So I did. Wow. What an ego I must have.

If what I have done has angered or hurt you, I have no
defense. I am sorry. I hope you can take solace in the fact
that I am someone you can easily ignore and dismiss.
And that this little book is just a foolish little act of faith.

Love,
A believer

Love, Amor, Ai,

Mohabbat, Ài,

Pasada hai, Hubun,

Amore, Anpu, Amor,

Muhabbat, Yêu,

Liebe, Lyublyu,

Prema, Aejeong,

Amour, Ask, Rak,

Hkyithkyinnmayt-

tar, Tresna, Lyubov.

I love them that love me, and those that seek
me earnestly shall find me.

— The Torah 

But of all I could name, verily love is the
highest. Love and devotion that make one
forgetful of everything else, Love that
unites the lover with me.

— The Bhagavad Gita 

LET LOVE AND
FAITHFULNESS
NEVER LEAVE
YOU;

BIND THEM
AROUND YOUR
NECK, WRITE THEM
ON THE TABLET OF
YOUR HEART.

— The Bible

In the Way of
Heaven, there is
no partiality of
love; it is always
on the side of
the good man.

– The Tao Te Ching

In the end, only three things matter:
how much you loved, how gently you lived,
and how gracefully you let go of things not
meant for you.

— The Tripitaka 

Love others as you would love yourself, judge
others as you would judge yourself, cherish
others as you would cherish yourself. When
you wish for others as you wish for yourself
and when you protect others as you would
protect yourself, that's when you can say it's
true love.

— The Analects 

Three things which are exceedingly good in
regard to the heavenly good spirits. And these
are as follows: Love and veneration and hope.

— The Denkard 

Let the Fear of God be your feet, and let His
Love be your hands; let His Understanding
be your eyes.

— The Guru Granth Sahib 

However men
try to reach me,
I return their
love with my
love; whatever
path they may
travel, it leads
to me in the end.

— The Bhagavad Gita

Just as a mother
would protect
her only child
with her life,

even so, let one
cultivate a
boundless love
towards all
beings.

— The Tripitaka

Only by undistracted love can men see me,
and know me, and enter into me.

— The Bhagavad Gita 

The foreigner residing among you must be
treated as your native-born. Love them as
yourself, for you were foreigners in Egypt.
I am the Lord your God.

— The Bible ✝

But I tell you, love your enemies and pray for those who persecute you.

— The Bible 

And it shall be offered, too, unto the poor from among those who, before them, had their abode in this realm and in faith - those who love all that come to them in search of refuge, and who harbor in their hearts no grudge for whatever the others may have been given, but rather give them preference over themselves, even though poverty be their own lot: for, such as from their own covetousness are saved - it is they, they that shall attain to a happy state!

— The Quran 

My mind is imbued with the Lord's Love; it is dyed a deep crimson. Truth and charity are my white clothes.

— The Guru Granth Sahib

THIS IS HOW WE KNOW WHAT LOVE IS: JESUS CHRIST LAID DOWN HIS LIFE FOR US. AND WE OUGHT TO LAY DOWN OUR LIVES FOR OUR BROTHERS AND SISTERS.

— The Bible

Those who do not know the way of love are foolish; they wander lost and confused.

— The Guru Granth Sahib 

I am he, whose thoughts are good, He, whose words are good, He, whose deeds are good .... Good thoughts, good words and good deeds are my food; and I love those of them who are in that place through good thoughts, good words and good deeds.

— The Denkard 

Love must be sincere. Hate what is evil; cling to what is good.

— The Bible 

The Lord casts His Glance of Grace, and inspires love and affection.

— The Guru Granth Sahib 

THE ONLY WAY YOU
CAN CONQUER ME
IS THROUGH LOVE
AND THERE
I AM GLADLY
CONQUERED.

— The Bhagavad Gita

WHEN MEN LOVE
AND HELP ONE
ANOTHER TO
THE BEST OF
THEIR POWER,
THEY DERIVE
THE GREATEST
PLEASURE FROM
LOVING THEIR
FELLOW-MEN.

— The Denkard

Love is patient, love is kind. It does not envy, it does not boast, it is not proud.

— The Bible ✝

I am the same to all beings, and my love is ever the same; but those who worship me with devotion, they are in me and I am in them.

— The Bhagavad Gita 

O mind, how can you be saved without love?

— The Bhagavad Gita 

Do everything in love.

— The Bible 

Hatred stirreth up strifes; but love covereth all transgressions.

— The Torah 

ONE MUST GUIDE
MANKIND TO THE
OCEAN OF TRUE
UNDERSTANDING
IN A SPIRIT OF LOVE
AND TOLERANCE.

— The Kitáb-i-Aqdas

It is easy to hate
and it is difficult
to love.

This is how the
whole scheme
of things works.
All good things
are difficult to
achieve;

and bad things are
very easy to get.

— The Analects

Whosoever loves every object of the Creator,
is a suppressor of his own failings, possesses
well-qualified prudence and intuitive wisdom,
and shares in the awards of the good religion.

— The Denkard 

Above all, love each other deeply, because
love covers over a multitude of sins.

— The Bible 

Therefore he who would administer the
kingdom, honoring it as he honors his own
person, may be employed to govern it, and he
who would administer it with the love which
he bears to his own person may be
entrusted with it.

— The Tao-te Ching 

Radiate boundless love towards the entire
world — above, below, and across —
unhindered, without ill will, without enmity.

— The Tripitaka 

LET NO DEBT REMAIN
OUTSTANDING, EXCEPT
THE CONTINUING
DEBT TO LOVE ONE
ANOTHER, FOR
WHOEVER LOVES
OTHERS HAS
FULFILLED THE LAW.

— The Bible

BETTER IS A
DINNER OF HERBS
WHERE LOVE IS,
THAN A STALLED
OX AND HATRED
THEREWITH.

— The Torah

Make your intellect your instrument, and love
your tambourine.

— The Guru Granth Sahib 

The only thing that counts is faith expressing
itself through love.

— The Bible ✝

He who has no attachments can really Love
others, for his love is pure and divine.

— The Bhagavad Gita 

A new command I give you: Love one
another. As I have loved you, so you must
love one another.

— The Bible 

ANGER BEGETS
MORE ANGER,
AND FORGIVENESS
AND LOVE LEAD
TO MORE
FORGIVENESS
AND LOVE.

— The Agamas

VERILY, THOSE WHO ATTAIN TO FAITH AND DO RIGHTEOUS DEEDS WILL THE MOST GRACIOUS ENDOW WITH LOVE.

— The Quran

We love because he first loved us.

— The Bible ✝

That cloak is true, which is dyed in the
color of the Love of my Beloved;
wearing it, my inner thirst is quenched.

— The Guru Granth Sahib 

Do everything you have to do, but not with
greed, not with ego, not with lust, not with
envy but with Love, compassion, humility
and devotion.

— The Bhagavad Gita 

Thou shalt not take vengeance, nor bear any
grudge against the children of thy people, but
thou shalt love thy neighbor as thyself:
I am the LORD.

— The Torah

HATRED DOES NOT
CEASE THROUGH
HATRED AT ANY
TIME. HATRED
CEASES THROUGH
LOVE. THIS IS AN
UNALTERABLE LAW.

— The Tripitaka

Ye are the dawning-places of the love of God and the daysprings of His loving kindness

— The Kitáb-i-Aqdas

This love has now become very strong; it has burnt away other corruption.

— The Guru Granth Sahib 

The commandments, "You shall not commit adultery," "You shall not murder," "You shall not steal," "You shall not covet," and whatever other command there may be, are summed up in this one command: "Love your neighbor as yourself."

— The Bible

Come, let us take our fill of love until the
morning; let us solace ourselves with loves.

— The Torah 

To rank the effort above the prize may be
called love.

— The Analects 

AND SPEND
FREELY IN GOD'S
CAUSE, AND LET
NOT YOUR OWN
HANDS THROW
YOU INTO
DESTRUCTION;
AND PERSEVERE IN
DOING GOOD:
BEHOLD, GOD
LOVES THE DOERS
OF GOOD.

— The Quran

THEY HELD EVEN
THIS THUS:

NAMELY,
LOVE ALL;

THAT SHOULD
BE WISDOM FOR
THEE.

— The Denkard

True Love cannot be broken, O Beloved;
throughout the ages, it remains.

— The Guru Granth Sahib 

If I have the gift of prophecy and can fathom
all mysteries and all knowledge, and if I have
a faith that can move mountains, but do not
have love, I am nothing.

— The Bible

Sing, and listen, and let your mind be filled
with love.

— The Guru Granth Sahib 

You can search throughout the entire universe for someone who is more deserving of your love and affection than you are yourself, and that person is not to be found anywhere. You, yourself, as much as anybody in the entire universe, deserve your love and affection.

— The Tripitaka 

To love a thing means wanting it to live.

— The Analects

Love, Amor, Ai,

Mohabbat, Ài,

Pasada hai, Hubun,

Amore, Anpu, Amor,

Muhabbat, Yêu,

Liebe, Lyublyu,

Prema, Aejeong,

Amour, Ask, Rak,

Hkyithkyinnmayt-

tar, Tresna, Lyubov.

My Dear Reader,

It's me again. I hope you got something out of this little book. I got a lot out of making it. Maybe while you were reading (or skimming, or just happened to see this book on someone's shelf) you read something that made you feel something.

If I am lucky — and this did happen once or twice — then please go explore the context and meaning of the passage. It's easy. You'll be glad you did.

Love,
A Believer

Bibliography

The Kitáb-i-Aqdas
bahai.org

THE Analects
classics.mit.edu

The Torah
mechon-mamre.org

The Bhagavad Gita
bhagavadgita.io

The Tao Te Ching
classics.mit.edu

The Denkard
avesta.org

The Quran
islamicity.org

The Agamas
sacred-texts.com

The Bible
biblegateway.com

The Tripitaka
accesstoinsight.org

The Guru Granth Sahib
srigranth.org

Public Domain Images
commons.wikimedia.org

www.ingramcontent.com/pod-product-compliance
Lightning Source LLC
Chambersburg PA
CBHW061441050726
47637CB00002B/7